The Complete BBQ Cookbook #2020

Quick and Delicious Barbecue Recipes for Beginners and Pro's incl. Desserts, Dips and Side Dishes

Jamie Webber

Copyright © [2020] [Jamie Webber]

All rights reserved

All rights for this book here presented belong exclusively to the author.
Usage or reproduction of the text is forbidden and requires a clear consent of the
author in case of expectations.

ISBN- 9798663373210

Table of Contents

INTRODUCTION 7

BARBECUE GRILL MAINTENANCE 11

MEAT RECIPES 12

    RECIPE 1: STICKY HOISIN RIBS 13

    RECIPE 2: HERBY LAMB KEBABS 16

    RECIPE 3: CHICHINGA – SUYA GOAT KEBABS 18

    RECIPE 4: CHICKEN SOUVLAKI 20

    RECIPE 5: SPATCHCOCK PIRI-PIRI CHICKEN 23

    RECIPE 6: CIDER CAN SOY-GLAZED DUCK 25

    RECIPE 7: GRIDDLED STEAK SANDWICH WITH OLIVE & CAPER BUTTER 27

    RECIPE 8: KOREAN CHILLI, SESAME & HONEY CHICKEN 28

    RECIPE 9: TRAFFIC LIGHT CHICKEN SHISH KEBABS 30

    RECIPE 10: PINEAPPLE & PORK SKEWERS 32

    RECIPE 11: NEXT-LEVEL BBQ CHICKEN 33

    RECIPE 12: ITALIAN CHICKEN SKEWERS 36

    RECIPE 13: SHORTCUT BBQ RIBS 37

    RECIPE 14: GRILLED KOREAN FLANK STEAK WITH SPICY CUCUMBER SALAD . 38

    RECIPE 15: GRILLED SKIRT STEAK WITH BLISTERED TOMATOES AND GUACAMOLE 40

    RECIPE 16: Steak Fajita Skewers 42

    RECIPE 17: GREEK CHICKEN KEBABS WITH TZATZIKI SAUCE 43

    RECIPE 18: JALAPEÑO-MARINATED GRILLED PORK CHOPS 45

    RECIPE 19: LEMON PEPPER CHICKEN KEBABS 47

RECIPE 20: GRILLED STEAKS WITH GARLIC CHIVE BUTTER AND FRENCH-STYLE POTATO SALAD 49

FISH & SEAFOOD RECIPES 51

RECIPE 21: FISH TACOS WITH GREEN JALAPEÑO SALSA & CHILLI CREAM 52
RECIPE 22: FISH WITH CHILLI, MANGO & LIME SALSA 54
RECIPE 23: SEAFOOD, PINEAPPLE & COCONUT KEBABS 56
RECIPE 24: SKEWERED SARDINES WITH TARTARE DRESSING 57
RECIPE 25: BARBECUED MUSSELS 58
RECIPE 26: MACKEREL WITH SIZZLED GARLIC, GINGER & TOMATOES 60
RECIPE 27: TIKKA-STYLE FISH 61
RECIPE 28: GRILLED WILD SALMON WITH ANCHOVIES, CAPERS & LENTILS 62
RECIPE 29: GRILLED SALMON TERIYAKI WITH CUCUMBER SALAD 64
RECIPE 30: BAKED SEA BASS WITH LEMONGRASS & GINGER 66

BURGER RECIPES 68

RECIPE 31: SOUTHWEST BURGERS 69
RECIPE 32: JALAPENO SWISS BURGERS 70
RECIPE 33: CLASSIC GRILLED BURGERS 71
RECIPE 34: BBQ BURGERS 72
RECIPE 35: BOLD HONEY-BARBECUE BURGER 74
RECIPE 36: CAJUN CHICKEN & PINEAPPLE BURGER 76
RECIPE 37: SMOKY MUSHROOM BURGERS WITH ROASTED GARLIC MAYO 77
RECIPE 38: HARISSA TURKEY BURGERS 79
RECIPE 39: ROSEMARY & GARLIC LAMB BURGER 81
RECIPE 40: BARBECUED BURGERS 82

BARBECUE SAUCE RECIPES 84

RECIPE 41: ST. LOUIS BARBECUE SAUCE 85
RECIPE 42: TEXAS BBQ SAUCE 86
RECIPE 43: SOUTHERN BARBECUE SAUCE 88

RECIPE 44: BBQ RUM SAUCE 89
RECIPE 45: BEST BBQ SAUCE 90
RECIPE 46: BARBECUE SAUCE 91
RECIPE 47: ALABAMA WHITE BBQ SAUCE 92
RECIPE 48: SWEET AND SMOKE HOMEMADE BBQ SAUCE 93
RECIPE 49: BBQ SAUCE – WITHOUT KETCHUP 94
RECIPE 50: GRAPE JELLY BBQ SAUCE - APPLE JELLY BBQ SAUCE 95

DESSERT & SNACK RECIPES 96

RECIPE 51: GRILLED PEACH MELBA 97
RECIPE 52: ROAST WHOLE PINEAPPLE WITH BLACK PEPPER & RUM 98
RECIPE 53: GRILLED DONUT ICE CREAM SANDWICHES 99
RECIPE 54: GRILLED PINEAPPLE SUNDAES 100
RECIPE 55: SPANISH MELON WITH SERRANO HAM 101

VEGETARIAN RECIPES 102

RECIPE 56: SWEET POTATOES WITH RED PEPPER & HALLOUMI 103
RECIPE 57: GRIDDLED VEGETABLES WITH MELTING AUBERGINES 104
RECIPE 58: BUTTER-BASTED BBQ CABBAGE 106
RECIPE 59: BARBECUE SESAME SWEET POTATOES 107
RECIPE 60: BARBECUE BAKED SWEET POTATOES 108

INTRODUCTION

Barbecued meals are great for summertime! And if you are reading this, then you are ready to have so much fun creating the sixty amazing recipes we have put together to make your Barbecue experience the very best! We have created recipes for meat, seafood, sauces, desserts and vegetarian meals!

However, before we go into the recipes, let us look at the tools and ways to manage your grills because these are the babies that help us make magic!

Barbecue Grills come in varieties such as the charcoal grills, the gas-fueled grills and the electric grills. There would no point to place on above the other because each has variety comes with its own benefits. However, we would provide brief insights into each grill type.

Charcoal Grills:

These have been around the longest and they are largely a favorite many people for reasons such as, the ease to use, and the smoky, rich flavor that only charcoal grills can give a meal. For all charcoal grills, regardless of the producer, there are a large number of similarities in the basic structure.

For starters, in such grills, air intake is manually adjusted and located towards the bottom of the grill and is adjusted manually. And the more air that is allowed to enter and exit the grill, the hotter the grill gets. This in itself is a benefit because the grill's temperature stabilizes based on the temperature zone you are cooking within. Typically, it remains constant and consistent throughout the cooking process, so long there is enough charcoal to keep it running at that temperature. This is an added benefit when cooking tougher meat cuts for long periods of time because it gives it more time to make the meat more tender and enhance its flavors.

Charcoal Kettle Grills:

Kettle grills are a type of Charcoal Grills and they are the most popular ones, due to their simple shape, the fact that they require a lot less charcoal to use and their portability. Shaped like a kettle, hence the name, they have a rounded bottom, a tight and removable lid, they come with sturdy stands, and grill grates. Here, the charcoal goes in the bottom of the grill, and it is raised on a small grate that allows any form of cooking dirt to fall freely away from the heat source and maintain a balanced airflow over the coals.

Kamado Grills

Often called egg grills or ceramic smokers, these fall into a category of more sophisticated charcoal grills; and in the past decade they have become very popular. They operate the same way Kettle grills, with only a few distinct differences. The Kamado Grill is shaped like an egg, it is heavier and is made from a thicker ceramic material so they weight can be anything from between 150-500 pounds.

However, just like the Kettle Grill, both temperature and air flow are regulated through the bottom and top, but due to its thermal mass and its slightly more engineered design, the slightest adjustment could significantly impact temperature changes. Also, due to its thickness and weight, its lid is not often removed and it is connected to the grill's base with heavy duty, spring-loaded hinges. Also, for this grill, once the charcoal has been fired, the grill would typically pre-heat for between 45 minutes to an hour. This allows it bring its thick walls as close to your desired temperature before cooking commences.

Pellet Grills

These have been out for about 3decades now but they have only become very popular in the past couple of years due to their convenience and their flavorful option. Another appealing thing about this grill is that it is also a smoker and is the perfect hybrid. It works a bit differently, and based on your desired temperature, both the burn pot and the thermostat work electronically to keep the grill close to this desired temperature. For the Pellet Grill, food-quality wood pellets about the size of a black-eyed pea are loaded into a hopper and are delivered to a burn pot with an auger.

It is convenient, especially with longer meals like large roasts, brisket and ribs, because it allows you cook the meat without extensive monitoring. Also, due to the electronic settings, it requires a power source and must be connected throughout the entire cook and cool-down process. These grills do not sear meat as effectively as other grills though, though this might be changing.

Gas and Propane Grills

Natural gas and propane grills are another very popular category of grills and it helps that there are so many styles to choose from. They operate similarly and have burners that emit around 40,000 BTUs of heat. And they are firing on three, four, or more burners to cook your food from below with either direct or indirect heat. One of their greatest appeals is that they are very convenient, heat up quickly and can come with many accessory options to improve the cooking experience. These accessories include side integrated food thermometers, burners, lights, and dedicated meat searing areas.

BARBECUE GRILL MAINTENANCE

Cleaning your Barbecue Grill after each use is not the only way to maintain it. You must remember that the same cooking activities that give you those wonderful meals, also produces carbon deposits on every surface of your grill, such as the hood, the firebox's interior, the favorizing bars and the burner tubes if you are using a gas grill. These carbon deposits ruin everything, they are ugly and when sugary sauces and grease stick to them, bacteria will grow. Also, the grill would eventually begin to heat unevenly and not operate properly. In a short while, it would prematurely fail.

So, to make it easy for you to clean your grills, here are must-follow steps throughout the summer, when you would be using the Barbecue Recipes we have provided in this book.

- Arm yourself with the right grill-cleaning tools. Starting with a long-handled wire brush, a five-gallon bucket, some elbow grease and a wire bottle brush.
- Avoid using toxic chemicals to clean your grills. This is because they can negatively affect the taste of your meals. Instead use warm water, grease-cutting dish soaps, baking soda and white vinegar as cleaning agents.
- Scrub the grill gates with a wire brush to clean it properly at the end of every barbecue session. Before every cooking session, make sure that you remove any loose wire-brush bristles before firing up the grill.

MEAT RECIPES

RECIPE 1: STICKY HOISIN RIBS

INGREDIENTS

- Olive Oil
- Oranges (2)
- Garlic (1 bulb)
- Jasmine Rice (450g//16oz)
- Hoisin Sauce (290ml//1 cup)
- Teaspoons of Chinese five-spice (2tsp//1 1/2tsp)
- 1 bunch of Fresh Rosemary or thyme (30g//1oz) - optional
- 4 Racks of higher-welfare baby back pork ribs (1.5-2kg//3-4lb)

FOR THE SALAD

- Fennel (1 bulb)
- Radishes (1 bunch)
- Piece of ginger (4 cm)
- Spring Onions (1 bunch)
- Fresh mixed-color chillies (3)
- 1 bunch of fresh coriander (30g//1oz)
- Low-salt soy sauce (1tsp//0.8tsp)
- Sesame oil (3tbsp//2 1/2tbsp imperial)
- 1 tablespoon rice wine vinegar (1tbsp//0.8tbsp imperial)

STEPS

1. Make sure you preheat the oven to 160°C/325°F/Gas 3.
2. On the ribs, lightly sprinkle a good pinch of the five-spice, the black pepper and the sea salt. Then drizzle a tbsp of olive oil over it before rubbing them all together. Put the ribs together in a large roasting tray before breaking apart the garlic bulb and scatter the unpeeled cloves over the ribs, then halve the oranges before adding them.
3. Now, using tin foil, cover the tray tightly and roast it all in the middle of the oven for approximately 3 hours, or until it is tender enough and thoroughly cooked.
4. Now for the salad, start by trimming the fennel, the radishes and the spring onions. Deseed the chillies and slice them lengthways, and make sure that they are sliced finely. Place the deseeded chillies in a bowl of ice-cold water to ensure it becomes super-crisp. At this point, pick in the coriander leaves and put them aside.
5. Prepare a quick salad dressing by mixing the soy, the sesame oil and the rice wine vinegar together. The ginger should be peeled and grated to become fine, now add black pepper to taste and season to get your desired result.
6. Remove the tray from the oven and move the ribs to a board. Carefully squeeze the sticky orange juice back into the tray then also carefully squeeze the soft garlic flesh out of the skins and mash it up. Scrape all the sticky bits from the tray. Place the tray over a medium heat on the hob or over your barbecue, let it start to bubble, then pour in the hoisin sauce. Let it stay for a few minutes, or at least until it is thick and shiny, before you remove it.
7. Dunk the rack of ribs one-by-one into the glaze and use your woody herbs as a brush to coat them generously all over and transfer to the

cool side of the barbecue as you finish with each. Cook them for about 10 more minutes or so, make sure they are covered while the air valve is open.

8. For the Jasmine Rice, cook according to the packet instructions. After this, fluff up and divide between your plates. Dry and drain the salad, then toss with the dressing and put into plates. Place the sticky ribs on top in a pile and enjoy!

EXTRA TIPS

- For the salad dressing, you can switch rice wine vinegar with fresh lime juice
- Sprinkling crushed nuts or sesame seeds on the ribs makes them extra delicious.
- If you want some extra smokiness, then add some wood chips or even woody herbs to the barbecue.
- If you are using your barbecue hob for something else, this recipe can be finished in the oven. Simply turn the heat up to 200°C/400°F/gas 6 and cook for about 8 to 10 minutes, making sure to regularly brush the ribs with the hoisin.

RECIPE 2: HERBY LAMB KEBABS

INGREDIENTS

- Lemon (1)
- Fresh mint (½ bunch)
- Extra Virgin Olive Oil
- Large Red Onions (2)
- Ripe Cherry Tomatoes (200g//7oz)
- Fat-Free natural yoghurt (300g//1½ cup)

- Quality lean lamb, such as Leg, Loin and Cannon (600g//1.3lb)
- Wooden Skewers (or use 8 long woody sprigs of fresh rosemary for that woody feel/essence)

FOR THE MARINADE

- Olive Oil
- Lemon (1)
- Fennel Seeds (2 Big Pinches)
- 1 large handful of wild garlic leaves or 3 cloves of garlic

STEPS

1. To make the marinade, start by tearing the wild garlics or peeling the garlic cloves. Then pound in a mortar with the fennel seeds, some black pepper and some seas salt. Remove from the mortar and mx the result with the lemon zest and about 80ml of olive oil, or until you can get the perfect consistency to coat the lamb with.
2. If you are making use of rosemary skewers then remove the leaves, leaving only those that are 2cm from the top. Sharpen both ends of the stick to enable you pierce the meat. Or if you are using wooden skewers, soak it in warm water for nothing less than 20minutes before making use of them.
3. The lamb should be cut into 5cm pieces. Now, peel and slice each onion into 6wedges before placing it in a large baking tray. The cherry tomatoes should be added. Mix with the marinade. The alternating ingredients should be threaded onto the skewers and refrigerated until it is ready to cook.
4. The mint leaves should be picked and finely chopped, then the yoghurt should be mixed, adding a squeeze of lemon juice, a pinch of salt and pepper, and a splash of the extra virgin olive oil. Serve this up with a drizzle of extra virgin olive oil, the minty yoghurt and a squeeze of lemon juice.

RECIPE 3: CHICHINGA – SUYA GOAT KEBABS

INGREDIENTS

FOR THE KEBABS

- Large Red Onion (1)
- Groundnut or Vegetable Oil
- Fresh Coriander (a few sprigs)
- Red, Green or Yellow Peppers – mixed colors if possible (1-2)
- Higher-welfare boneless leg of a kid goat – diced (450g//1lb)

FOR THE SPICE RUB

- Ginger (5cm)
- Cloves of Garlic (3)
- Smoked Paprika (5ml//1tsp)
- Roasted Peanuts (125g//4.4oz)
- Groundnut Oil or Vegetable Oil (30ml//2tbsp)
- Cayenne pepper or red chilli flakes – for extra heat (2ml//1tsp)

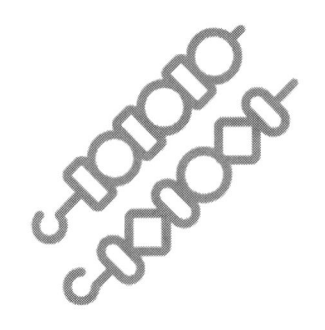

STEPS

1. Pound the Peanuts, making sure to keep them fairly coarse. Reserve a small handful to serve and place the nuts in a large bowl. Peel and grate the garlic and ginger (if the ginger is organic, keep the skin on), add the remaining ingredients for the spice rub, a teaspoon of coarse black pepper and a pinch of sea salt.
2. Add the diced goat and massage thoroughly into the meat. Peel the red onion and slice into quarters, deseed it and cut the peppers into chunks. Thread the goat meat, peppers and onions onto the skewers. Remember that the longer you allow you meat marinate, the between it would be. So, if you have enough time, leave the skewers in the fridge for about 1-2 hours or even overnight.
3. Remove the skewers from the fridge and sit them at room temperature for a few minutes while you make the grill or griddle pan hot. Moisten the meat with black pepper, sea salt and a little oil before putting it under the grill or on the griddle – it should sizzle but you must not move it. Only turn it every 2 minutes, and do so until every side is seared through (that is if you are going for medium-rare). If you are going for well-done, then turn every 3 minutes.
4. Allow these to rest for up to 2minutes, then scatter over the reserved peanuts and add a small pinch of chilli powder. Tear the coriander leaves over and serve with a fresh seasonal salad. Now enjoy!

RECIPE 4: CHICKEN SOUVLAKI

INGREDIENTS

FOR THE MARINADE

- Coriander (1/3 tbsp// 1tsp)
- Olive Oil (4tbsp)
- Dried Mint (1tsp)
- Crushed Garlic (4)
- Sweet Paprika (1tsp)
- Ground Cumin (1tsp//1/3 tbsp)
- Dried Oregano (1/8cup//2tbsp)
- Ground Cinnamon (½tsp)
- Zest & Juice from 1 lemon
- 1 lemon cut into wedges – to serve

FOR THE PITTA WRAPS

- Golden Caster Sugar (1tsp)
- Strong White Bread Flour (250g//9oz)
- Fast-Action Dried Yeast (7g//0.24oz sachet)
- Olive Oil (2tsp), remember to keep some extra for greasing the chicken

FOR THE TZATZIKI

- Cucumber (½)
- Greek yogurt (200g//7oz)
- Lemon Juice (½sized lemon)
- 1 small garlic clove, crushed
- Bunch mint, finely chopped (small-sized)

TO SERVE

- 1 butter or round lettuce

- 4 large tomatoes, deseeded and chopped
- 1 red onion, halved and thinly sliced

TOOLS YOU WOULD NEED

- 4 long metal skewers

STEPS

1. Place the chicken in a large bowl and add the ingredients for the marinade. Also add plenty of black pepper and just 1tsp of salt. Mix these well ensuring that each thigh is well-coated with the marinade. Cover this and chill for at least 3hours or even up to 48hours if you have all that time to spend.
2. Now, a few hours before you are ready to eat, start making the Pitta. In a bowl, mix the sugar, the yeast, the flour, and use your fingers to sprinkle ½ tsp of salt. Now add 150ml/over half a cup of lukewarm water and 2tsp of olive oil then combine to a dough.
3. Tip this onto a work surface and knead this for about 8-10minutes (or if you have a tabletop mixer, you can get this done in 5minutes). Clean the bowl then oil it. Return the dough and make sure you cover it loosely with cling film. Allow to rise for an hour or until it has been doubled in size. Separate the dough into four equal pieces and roll out into circles, making sure to keep them as thin as possible. Cover these with sheets of oiled cling firm and allow to rise for about 15-20 mins.
4. Now, to make the Tzatziki, we cut the cucumber lengthways into halves and deseed it. Finely chop these before combining with the remaining ingredients, now add a pinch of salt.

TO MAKE THE TZATZIKI,

1. Cut the cucumber into two equal parts lengthways and scoop out the seeds. Finely chop, then combine with the remaining ingredients, along with a pinch of salt. Chill until ready to serve.
2. Heat the grill to its highest setting. Line a roasting tin with foil and find 4 metal skewers long enough to sit across the top with a little space underneath. Remove the chicken from the fridge, take one thigh and thread it over 2 skewers, so it has a skewer through either side. Place another chicken on top and leave a small gap between each piece of chicken, ensuring that you can eventually fit 6 thighs of chicken on each pair of skewers. Position the skewers on top of the roasting tin and set aside while you finish the pittas.
3. Heat a large frying pan (or two if you have them) over a medium-high heat and brush the breads with oil. Gently lift one into the pan. It should sizzle, and bubbles should appear on the surface after 1-2 mins. When the underside is golden, flip it and cook for another 2-3 mins. Continue doing this until you have cooked all the breads, make sure that as you go, you also wrap them in a foil. Let the bread remain warm in the bottom of the oven while you cook the chicken. Alternatively, cook on the barbecue for 5-8 mins, turning occasionally.
4. Place the chicken under the hot grill and allow to cook for about 15 to 20 mins, occasionally brush it with the oil and any other juices that you will find at the bottom of the tin. Turn the chicken turning halfway through cooking, and once it is cooked, remove it from the oven and allow to rest for 5minutes.
5. Cut through each pair of skewers to make four kebabs and serve in the warm bread, with lettuce, tomato, red onion, lemon wedges and tzatziki.

RECIPE 5: SPATCHCOCK PIRI-PIRI CHICKEN

INGREDIENTS

- Olive Oil (1/2cup//2tbsp)
- Garlic Cloves, crushed (3)
- Tabasco Sauce – optional
- Lemon Wedges – optional
- Sweet Paprika (10ml//2tsp)
- 1 Chicken (1½ kg//3.3lb)
- Chopped Parsley (30ml//2tbsp)
- Red wine Vinegar (30ml//2tbsp)
- Red Chillies, chopped; deseed it if you want it a lot less spicy (4)

STEPS

1. Firstly, you would have to spatchcock the chicken, to do this, flip it over so the backbone is facing you. Then use a pair of kitchen scissors – make sure they are sturdy – and cut down either side of the chicken's backbone, then discard this. Turn the chicken over and then firmly push down on the breastbone to flatten out the bird. Carefully make a couple of slashes in each leg joint.
2. Now, take the chillies and garlic and put them in a food processor, add a pinch of salt to taste too, or you could make use of a pestle and mortar if you do not own/want to use a food processor. Blend/Pound this to paste, and add the olive oil, paprika, vinegar and parsley. Mix all these well then smear it over the kitchen. Leave them to marinate for at least an hour and if you can leave it overnight, then do so. The chicken can be frozen at this point too.
3. Fire up the barbecue and when the flames have died down, place the chicken at the centre of the barbecue. The skin-side should face down, and cook this for at least 15-20 minutes or until it is nicely charred. Flip the chicken over and continue cooking each side for another 5-15 mins until it is thoroughly cooked through. Be sure that the juices run clear because heat varies from barbecue to barbecue.
4. If you are using an oven, heat to 180C-200C fan/gas 6 and cook and cook for 35-40 mins on a baking tray. To burn the skin, roast for a further 5-10 mins.
5. Serve with lemon wedges, and if you like it hot, serve with Tabasco.

RECIPE 6: CIDER CAN SOY-GLAZED DUCK

INGREDIENTS

- Honey (30ml//2tbsp)
- Sesame Oil (5ml//1tsp)
- Soy Sauce (100ml//6 1/2 tbsp)
- Garlic Cloves, finely sliced (2)
- 1 Whole Duck (between 2-2½ kg//4.4-5.5lb)
- Canned good-quality Cider (500ml)
- Sichuan pepper, crushed (10ml//2tsp)
- Chinese five-spice powder (5ml//1tsp)
- A bunch of coriander, to serve – optional
- 3 tbsp Chilli Sauce – ideal options are Sriracha or Sweet Chilli (3tbsp)

STEPS

1. Start off by lightly scoring the duck skin all over and rubbing with some salt and the five-spice, making sure you get into the cut marks – this can be done a day ahead to help you save time and ensure that you have time to leave it into marinate in the fridge, uncovered.

2. Light a lidded barbecue and allow the flames to die down, make sure that the coals also turn ashen and then mound it up on one side. If your barbecue is a small one, you must remove the grills and put a strong roasting tin on the barbecue floor right next to the coals – this will allow for space to close the lid once the duck is in the barbecue. If your barbecue is a large one, then the duck will sit in a tray directly on the grills. If you are using an oven, heat it to 180C/160C fan/gas 4.

3. Open the can of Cider, make sure you reserve a few tablespoons for the sauce, pour about half of the Cider into a glass. Add the garlic and ginger into the can first, then pour in the oil and half the soy. Place the duck leg down on the can, so that it is sitting upright with its cavity. Stand it upright on the tray in the barbecue or oven, close the lid and cook for 1 hr. Whisk the remaining chilli sauce, honey and soy with the cider that had been reserved. Brush the sauce all over the duck and cook for another hour, making sure to baste it every 10-15 minutes with all the sticky juices contained in the pan. Baste until the duck is glossy and sark.
4. Remove the duck from barbecue or oven and allow it to rest for 30minutes. Now, mix some flaky sea salt with the Sichuan pepper and carefully lift the duck off the tray and the can. Season the duck with the spiced salt and add the coriander to the cavity.
5. Carve, Serve and Enjoy!

RECIPE 7: GRIDDLED STEAK SANDWICH WITH OLIVE & CAPER BUTTER

INGREDIENTS

- Capers (3)
- Ciabatta loaf (½)
- Olive Oil (10ml//2tsp)
- Thyme Leave (a pinch)
- Pitted Olives, any color (2)
- Little Gem Lettuces Leaves (2)
- Butter, softened (15ml//1tbsp)
- Rump steak, trimmed of any fat (175g//6oz)

STEPS

1. Using a small bowl, mix the butter and the pepper. Finely chop the olives, the thyme leaves and the capers into this bowl and stir well. Chill this until it is ready to use. Heat up a girdle pan or a barbecue until it is smoking, brush up the steak with a little of the oil and lay it on the pan or the barbecue. Cook each side of the steak for 3-4 minutes. When this is cooked thoroughly, transfer it to a board and cover with foil to rest.
2. Cut the Ciabatta loaf in half and brush the cut side with oil. Place them cut-side down on the griddle pan for 1-2 mins, until charred. Put the steak on the bottom half of the loaf and spoon the butter over it. Add the lettuce leaves and sit the top of the loaf on

RECIPE 8: KOREAN CHILLI, SESAME & HONEY CHICKEN

INGREDIENTS

- Spring Onions, sliced (4)
- Soy Sauce (30ml//2tbsp)
- Sesame Oil (15ml//1tbsp)
- Ginger, grated (thumb-sized piece)
- Chicken Thighs, boneless and skinless (12)

FOR THE GLAZE

- Juice (½ lime)
- Honey (30ml//2tbsp)
- Sesame Oil (5ml//1tsp)
- Soy Sauce (15ml//1tbsp)
- Sesame Seeds (30ml//2 tbsp)
- Korean chilli paste, also known as gochujang (60ml//4tbsp) OR A mixture of Ketchup (45ml//3tbsp) and Sriracha Chilli Sauce (15ml//1tbsp)

STEPS

1. Mix the ginger, soy sauce and sesame oil and toss the chicken in this mix. Thread each chicken thigh on two long metal skewers, making sure that each skewer penetrates one side of the thigh. Thread the chicken, until it is tightly packed onto the skewers. Chill these until you're ready to cook and start mixing the ingredients for the glaze.
2. Fire up the BBQ and if you are using a coal BBQ, allow the coals to turn ashen before you start cooking. For 5-6minutes, cook each side of the kebab, note that the cooking time depends on the heat from the BBQ. Once the kebab is nicely charred but not fully cooked through, you should start painting on the glaze. Make sure it is not fully cooked through or cooked for too long else the honey will catch. Remember that the way to achieve a nice and sticky chicken is to start applying the glaze in layers, making sure to turn the kebab often.
3. As soon as the glaze has been used up, and the chicken has been thoroughly cooked, this should take approximately 20minutes in total, transfer the chicken to a plate and allow to cool for 5minutes before serving.
4. Serve, scattered with spring onions. Enjoy!

RECIPE 9: TRAFFIC LIGHT CHICKEN SHISH KEBABS

INGREDIENTS

- Warmed Flatbreads, chopped
- Tomato & Lemon Wedges, to serve
- Chicken Breasts, chopped into large chunks (6)
- Red, Orange & Green Peppers, deseeded and chopped into large chunks (2 of each)

FOR THE MARINADE AND SAUCE

- Paprika (15ml//1tbsp)
- Ketchup (45ml//3tbsp)
- Garlic Cloves, finely grated (2)
- Natural or Greek Yogurt (300g//11oz)

Tip: If you are using wooden skewers, then soak them in water for up to 1hour before you.

STEPS

1. In a large bowl, mix all the ingredients for the marinade together and spoon a third of this into a smaller bowl, cover and chill until needed. In the remaining marinade left in the large bowl, stir the chicken and set this aside for 20minutes. This can be covered and chilled for up to two days, so you can make both marinade and chicken ahead of time. Start threading the chicken and the peppers onto the skewers until you have up to 6 to 8 kebabs. This can also be prepared in advance, and you would have to chill the kebabs to preserve them.
2. Fire up the barbecue to medium heat, or until a thin layer of the coals have become grey. Cook the kebabs for 10 minutes and turn them occasionally, until all sides of the chicken have been charred and cooked thoroughly.
3. Now, you can serve the kebabs with the reserved yoghurt sauce (marinade), chopped tomatoes warmed flatbreads, and lemon wedges on the side.

RECIPE 10: PINEAPPLE & PORK SKEWERS

INGREDIENTS

- Cider Vinegar (600ml)
- Fish Sauce (15ml//1tsp)
- Pork Fillet (400g//1lb)
- Cooked rice or pitta – to serve
- Light Muscovado Sugar (50ml//4tbsp)
- Small bunch of Coriander, chopped – optional
- Spring Onions (4), trimmed and cut into 4 equal lengths
- Green Pepper, deseeded and cut into squares (1) – optional
- Small Pineapple, peeled, cored and cut into chunks (½) OR ready-prepped fresh pineapple, drained well

STEPS

1. Start with cutting the pork into cubes and heat up the vinegar and the sugar in a pan over a low heat until the sugar melts. Add the fish sauce to the pan and allow to cool. Now, add the pork and mix properly to ensure that all the cubes are covered in sauce.
2. Heat up the barbecue and if you are using coals, allow them to turn white; and if you are indoors, heat a griddle pan. Now, thread the skewers with the pineapple and pork, and put in alternating pieces of spring onion and pepper. Griddle or barbecue each side of the skewers for up to 3-4minutes, note that you might need to cook them for longer if you are using a griddle pan.
3. To serve, sprinkle with coriander, and with rice or slide them into pitta breads.

RECIPE 11: NEXT-LEVEL BBQ CHICKEN

INGREDIENTS

- Bay Leaf (1)
- Paprika (½tsp)
- Ketchup (200ml)
- Soy Sauce (60ml//4tbsp)
- Ground Cumin (5ml//1tsp)
- Chopped Thyme (30ml//2tbsp)
- Garlic Cloves, roughly chopped (8)
- Spring Onions, roughly chopped (8)
- Dark-Brown Soft Sugar (45ml//3tbsp)
- Mix of chicken drumsticks and wings, lightly scored (1½kg//3.3lb)
- Limes (4), 2 should be juiced and 2 should be halved to serve
- Red Chillies (2), tops removed and reserved for the smoke mix
- A thumb-sized piece of ginger, thoroughly peeled and roughly chopped

FOR THE SMOKE MIX (OPTIONAL)

- Reserved Chilli Tops
- Ground Allspice (5ml//1tsp)
- Handful of Bay Leaves
- Handful of Thyme Sprigs

STEPS

1. Start with preparing the meat. Put all the ingredients, except for the ketchup and the chicken, into a blender or a mini food processor. Add a pinch of salt and blitz to the rough paste. Pour two-thirds of the paste into a large bowl and add the chicken. Massage the marinade into the meat, cover and leave for at least 1hour at room temperature, or for up to 48hours in the fridge.
2. Now, make the barbecue sauce. Pour the remaining paste into a small saucepan and allow to simmer, then cook for 5minutes until it thickens and becomes darker. Add the ketchup and allow to cook for 5minutes until it becomes sticky. Pour this into a container and set aside.
3. Fire up the barbecue, making sure that the coals and placed at one end in a pile, leave only a few on the other side. Place the chicken on the emptier side and if you are making the smoke mix, be sure to carefully scatter all of the ingredients directly onto the piled-up coals. With the vents open, cover the barbecue and cook the chicken for up to 20minutes. Remove the barbecue lid and turn the chicken, before covering again and cooking for another 20minutes.
4. After 20minutes, open it and move the chicken across the grill placing it above the piled-up coals, and baste with some of the barbecue sauce, make sure to reserve some barbecue sauce for serving later. Cook for 10minutes and add a couple more coals if you necessary, also turn the chicken often until it is thoroughly cooked and nicely charred.

Tip: To get the perfect temperature, insert a digital thermometer into the thickest part of the meat, and it should read at least 65C. Put the cut-side of the lime halves on the grill, and specifically over the coals for 3-4 mins until it is charred. To serve, place the line for squeezing over and the reserve barbecue sauce for dipping.

RECIPE 12: ITALIAN CHICKEN SKEWERS

INGREDIENTS

- Kosher Salt
- Garlic Cloves, minced (3)
- Tomato Paste (30ml//2tbsp)
- Freshly ground black pepper
- Baguette French bread, cut into cubes (1)
- Wooden Skewers, soaked in water for 20 minutes (8)
- Extra-virgin olive oil, add extra for drizzling (4tbsp//1/4cup)
- Boneless Skinless Chicken Breasts, cut into large cubes (450g//1lb)
- Chopped Fresh Italian Parsley, add extra leaves for garnish (15ml//1tbsp)

STEPS

1. First, season your chicken with salt and pepper.
2. To make the Marinade: In a large bowl, combine the garlic cloves, the chopped parsley, the olive oil and the tomato paste. Put in the chicken and toss it toy ensure it gets fully coated with the marinade. Refrigerate this for only 30minutes.
3. Preheat the grill to medium-high heat and thread the bread and the chicken on the skewer. Drizzle this with olive oil and season with pepper and salt.
4. Grill the skewers, turning them often until the chicken is cooked through and bread is slightly charred, this should take about 10 minutes. To serve, garnish with parsley.

RECIPE 13: SHORTCUT BBQ RIBS

INGREDIENTS

- Kosher Salt
- Brown Sugar (3tbsp)
- Garlic Cloves, minced (4)
- Freshly ground black pepper
- Smoked Paprika (2tsp//10ml)
- Barbecue Sauce (16tbsp//1cup)
- 1 rack baby back ribs (about 1.3kg//3lb)

STEPS

1. Over medium-high heat, preheat the Grill Pan or the Grill and cut the ribs into 3 sections, at the same time. Using a large pot, add the ribs and fill it with enough water to cover the ribs. Add a tablespoon of salt, and allow this boil and simmer for 20minues. Drain the ribs and place them on a sheet pan. Using a paper towel, dry them well.
2. To make the Spice Rub. In a small bowl, put the brown sugar, the garlic, the 1 teaspoon of salt, the paprika and the 1/2 teaspoon of black pepper. Mix this and using a spoon, pour the mixture onto the ribs and rub all over with hands. Cook the ribs on a grill pan or a grill for up to 10minutes and turn it halfway through this time.
3. Now, brush the rubs with the barbecue sauce and cook for 1minute more until it is lightly charred. Serve the ribs with barbecue sauce and enjoy.

RECIPE 14: GRILLED KOREAN FLANK STEAK WITH SPICY CUCUMBER SALAD

INGREDIENTS

- Kosher Salt
- Sugar (5ml//1tsp)
- Honey (30ml//2tbsp)
- Garlic Cloves, minced (4)
- Flank Steak (465g//1lb)
- Cooked White Rice, for serving
- Sriracha, divided (45ml//3tbsp)
- Sliced Green Onions, for serving
- Sesame oil, divided (45ml//3tbsp)
- Rice Wine Vinegar, divided (1/2 cup)
- Freshly Minced Ginger (30ml//2tbsp)
- Vegetable oil (1/4 cups + 30ml//2tbsp)
- Crushed Red Pepper Flakes (5ml//1tsp)
- Low-Sodium Soy Sauce (1/2cups plus 1 tbsp)
- 2 large cucumbers, cut lengthwise, seeded, and thinly sliced

STEPS

1. Using a large bowl, mix the vegetable oil, half of the rice wine vinegar, honey, 2 tablespoons of Sriracha half cup of Soy Sauce, garlic, ginger and 2 tablespoons of Sesame Oil. Mix thoroughly and pour half of the sauce over the flank steak, leave to marinate for 10minutes and reserve the other half.
2. To make the boiled rice: Using a saucepan, boil rice and enough water. When it boils, reduce the heat and simmer, keeping it covered for 15minutes. Then, remove from heat and allow it sit, still covered, until it is ready to use. Before use, fluff it with a fork, season with salt and top with sesame seeds.
3. To make the cucumber salad: Using a large bowl, whisk the remaining rice wine vinegar, sesame oil, soy sauce, Sriracha, sugar, and red pepper flakes. Whisk thoroughly, then stir in the cucumbers and season with salt.
4. Over high heat, heat up a grill or grill pan. Season the steak with pepper and salt, then grill each side for 5 to 6 minutes for medium-rare. Place the steak on a cutting board and allow to rest for 5minutes, then thinly slice across the grain. Pour juices into a small bowl containing the remaining sauce and stir to mix well.
5. To serve, drizzle the steak with sauce and garnish with scallions. Serve with cucumber salad and rice.

RECIPE 15: GRILLED SKIRT STEAK WITH BLISTERED TOMATOES AND GUACAMOLE

INGREDIENTS

- Kosher Salt
- Avocados, diced (3)
- Cumin (10ml//2tsp)
- Coriander (5ml//1tsp)
- Lime Juice (50ml//4tbsp)
- Garlic Cloves, minced (2)
- Skirt Steak (465g//1lb)
- Freshly ground black pepper
- Crushed Red Pepper Flakes (1/2tsp)
- Red Grape Tomatoes, halved (3/4cups)
- 2 tbsp. finely chopped red onion (2tbsp)
- Yellow Grape Tomatoes, halved (3/4cups)
- Extra-Virgin Olive Oil, divided (45ml//3tbsp)
- Finely Chopped Fresh Cilantro, plus cilantro leaves for serving (2tbsp)

STEPS

1. Put the steak in a glass baking dish that is shallow.
2. In a small bowl, whisk together 2 tablespoons of lime juice and olive oil, the garlic, cumin, and the coriander. Pour this mixture over the steak, using this to coat it properly before marinating for 10minutes.
3. To make the guacamole: Using a medium-sized bowl, mash together the onions, avocado, cilantro, the red pepper flakes and the remaining 2 tablespoons of lime juice until the mixture is chunky. Then season it with salt. In another bowl, mix the tomatoes with what remains of the 1 tablespoon olive oil and season with salt and pepper to your desired taste.
4. Over medium-high heat, heat up a grill pan. Grill the tomatoes until they have been blistered, this should take about 4minutes. Then remove the tomatoes from the grill, and increase the heat to high. To the hot grill, add the steak and season with salt and pepper. Grill each side of the steak for up to 3minutes then allow to rest for 5minutes.
5. Now, thinly slice the steak against the grain, and top with cilantro and the blistered tomatoes. Serve with guacamole.

RECIPE 16: STEAK FAJITA SKEWERS

INGREDIENTS

- Kosher Salt
- Freshly ground black pepper
- Scallions, cut into thirds (1 bunch)
- Extra-virgin olive oil, for drizzling
- Large Bell Peppers, cut into large pieces (4)
- Skewers, soaked in water for 20 minutes (8)
- Sirloin Steak, cut into large cubes (450g//1lb)
- Small Flour Tortillas, torn into large pieces (1 pack)

STEPS

1. Preheat grill to medium-high. Skewer the tortillas (folded), the scallions, the steak, and the peppers. Drizzle with olive oil and season with salt and pepper to your desired taste. Grill, making sure to turn occasionally, until the steak is medium rare and vegetables tender and slightly charred, this should take about 7 minutes.

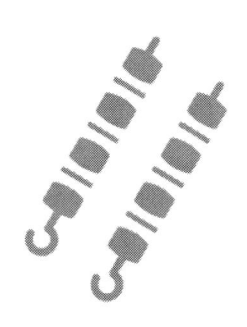

RECIPE 17: GREEK CHICKEN KEBABS WITH TZATZIKI SAUCE

INGREDIENTS

- Garlic Cloves, minced (3)
- Ground Coriander (1/2tsp)
- Dried Thyme (2.5ml//1/2tsp)
- Dried Basil, divided (11/2tsp)
- Red Wine Vinegar (15ml//1tbsp)
- Fresh Lemon Juice (45ml//3tbsp)
- Dried Oregano, divided (21/2tsp)
- Salt and freshly ground black pepper
- Large Red Onion, diced into 11/4" wedges (1)
- Large Red Bell Peppers, diced into 11/4" pieces (2)
- Olive Oil, divided, plus more for grill (1/4cup+ 2tbsp)
- Boneless Skinless Chicken Breasts, diced into 11/4" cubes (450g//1lb)
- 3 Small Zucchinis, sliced into rounds slightly under 1/2" thick (nearly 450g//1lb)

Tip: If using wooden skewers soak them in water for 30 minutes.

STEPS

FOR THE KEBABS:

1. Whisk together 1/4 cup of olive oil, 1 teaspoon of basil 2 tsp oregano, lemon juice, thyme, garlic, vinegar, and coriander. Sprinkle salt and pepper until you get your desired taste.
2. Place the chicken in a resealable gallon-size bag and pour the olive oil mixture over it. Make sure to press the chicken into the marinade. Close the bag lid and refrigerate for 45 minutes to 2 hours (no longer than 2 hours or the acidic ingredients will make the chicken mealy). Drizzle and toss the vegetables with 2tablespoons of the Olive Oil and season with the remaining 1/2 tsp basil, 1/2 tsp oregano, and salt to taste.
3. Preheat a grill over medium-high heat and thread a skewer with a dash of red bell pepper, red onion, zucchini, and 2 chicken pieces, make sure to repeat this process twice. Lightly brush the grill with olive oil and place the skewers there, grill until for about 8-12 minutes, or until the chicken registers 165°F (73°C) in centre, make sure you rotate once, halfway through cooking. When it is ready, garnish with parsley.
4. Serve warm with tzatziki sauce.

RECIPE 18: JALAPEÑO-MARINATED GRILLED PORK CHOPS

INGREDIENTS

- Kosher Salt
- Sugar (5ml//1tsp)
- Large Jalapeños (2)
- Freshly Ground Pepper
- Coriander Seeds (10ml//2tsp)
- Apple Cider Vinegar (4tbsp//1/4cup)
- Medium White Onion, very thinly sliced (1/4)
- Four bone-in-pork rib chops (about 300g//10oz each)
- Extra-Virgin Olive Oil, divided, plus more for grill (1/2cup + 3tbsp)

STEPS

1. Set up the grill at medium-heat and lightly oil the grate. Pat the pork chops dry and season them generously with salt and pepper, all over. Place the pork chops on a rimmed baking sheet and allow to sit at room temperature for between 30 minutes to a 1 hour.

2. To make the marinade: In a dry small skillet, toast coriander seeds over medium heat, making sure to toss often until they are golden brown and have a fragrance, this should take about 2minutes. Transfer the seeds to a cutting board and allow it to cool. Making use of a flat-bottomed mug or a heavy skillet, lightly crush the coriander seeds and place them in a small bowl. Now add sugar, vinegar, and half a cup of oil, season this with salt and pepper. Whisk the mixture until both the sugar and salt are dissolved. Set aside.

3. Toss the jalapeños and a tablespoon of oil into a small bowl and allow to coat, season this with salt and pepper. Pat the pork chops dry again, this is because the salt would have drawn out moisture, and rub with what is left of the 2tablespoons of Oil. Grill the jalapeños, turning them often, until they are softened and blackened in spots, this should take about 5 minutes.
4. Transfer the jalapeños to a cutting board. Grill the pork chops, and turn them every 2 minutes or so, until they are properly cooked but still at medium-rare closest to the bone (Tip: inserting a thermometer and getting a read of 145°F is a sure-fire way of getting the correct answer), this should take up to 8–12 minutes. Then transfer to cutting board and allow to rest 10–15 minutes.
5. Cut the pork chops along the bone to remove meat in one piece; slice 1/2" thick and transfer to a rimmed platter. Slice the jalapeños slanting into rounds and scatter over pork. Pour the marinade that had been reserved on it and allow to sit for between 15minutes to 1hour before serving.
6. To serve, scatter onion over

RECIPE 19: LEMON PEPPER CHICKEN KEBABS

INGREDIENTS

- Salt (5ml//1tsp)
- Olive Oil (4tbsp//1/4cup)
- Lemon Zest (10ml//2tsp)
- Garlic Cloves, minced (15ml//1tbsp)
- Minced Fresh Rosemary (15ml//1tbsp)
- Fresh Lemon Juice (1/4cup//4tbsp)
- Small Zucchinis, sliced into 1/4" thick disks (2)
- Large Red Onion, peeled and cut into wedges (1)
- Small Yellow Squash, sliced into 1/4" thick disks (2)
- Freshly Ground Black Pepper, add more to taste (7.5ml//11/2 tsp)
- Boneless Skinless Chicken Breasts, diced into 11/2" pieces (465g//1lb)

STEPS

Tip: If using wooden skewers soak in water at least 1 hour.

1. Using a mixing bowl whisk together the olive oil, rosemary, lemon juice & lemon zest, garlic, pepper and salt. Place the chicken breasts in a resealable gallon-size bag, and pour marinade over chicken. Seal the bag while pressing excess air out of it and rub the marinade all over the chicken. Transfer the chicken to the refrigerator and allow to rest for 1-2 hours.

2. Over medium-high heat, preheat the grill to about 425o and thread the squash, the zucchini, the chicken and the red onion onto skewers. Lightly oil the grates with oil (a brush will help here), and place the kebabs on the grill. Grill each side for about 5 minutes or until the chicken registers 165o on an instant read thermometer (this will help you with accuracy).
3. Season with more pepper as desired and serve warm.

RECIPE 20: GRILLED STEAKS WITH GARLIC CHIVE BUTTER AND FRENCH-STYLE POTATO SALAD

INGREDIENTS

- Kosher Salt
- Dijon mustard (1tsp)
- Small Shallot, minced (1/2)
- Freshly ground black pepper
- Extra-Virgin Olive Oil (1/4cup)
- Small Garlic Clove, minced (1)
- 10-oz. NY strip steaks, halved (2)
- Red Wine Vinegar (2tbsp//1/8cup)
- Small Red Potatoes (465g//1lb)
- Minced Chives, divided (45ml//3tbsp)
- Finely Chopped Fresh Basil (30ml//2tbsp)
- Finely Chopped Fresh Parsley (30ml//2tbsp)
- Unsalted Butter, room temperature (60ml//4tbsp//)
- Green Onions, halved lengthwise, white and light green parts thinly sliced (2)

STEPS

1. Boil the potatoes in a medium-sized pot until they are tender for 20minutes, then drain. When they are cool enough, cut them into quarters. Using a small bowl, combine 1 tablespoon chives, shallot, butter and garlic; season with salt and pepper to your desired taste. Cover this, and chill until ready to use.
2. In a large bowl, put in the red wine vinegar and the Dijon mustard and slowly whisk in the olive oil and season with salt and pepper. Add 2 tablespoons chives, the potatoes, parsley, green onions, and basil, and stir gently and thoroughly. Sprinkle with salt and pepper until you achieve your desired taste. Heat up a lightly oiled grill pan over high heat, and season the steaks with salt and pepper. Grill each side of the steak for 3 minutes until they are medium rare.
3. Place a dollop of chive butter on each steak and allow to rest a few minutes, then serve with the potato salad.

FISH & SEAFOOD RECIPES

RECIPE 21: FISH TACOS WITH GREEN JALAPEÑO SALSA & CHILLI CREAM

INGREDIENTS

- Red Onion (1)
- Sugar (1/6oz // 1tsp)
- Honey (5ml // 1tsp)
- Olive Oil (15ml // 1tbsp)
- Garlic Salt (1/6oz // 1tsp)
- Sliced Radishes, to serve
- Ground Cumin (1/6oz // 1tsp)
- Mild Chilli Powder (1/6oz // 1tsp)
- Shredded white cabbage, to serve
- Warmed soft corn tortillas, to serve
- Chipotle, Tabasco or another hot sauce, to serve
- Swordfish steaks or other firm white fish (500g // 1.1lb), cut into 3cm cubes
- Limes (zest of 2 and juice of 1), plus lime wedges to serve (save the other one for the salsa)

STEPS

1. Using a shallow dish, mix the fish with the Lime juice, Lime Zest, Olive Oil and Honey. Cover this and allow to marinate for up to 30minutes in the fridge. Using another small bowl, mix the spices together with sugar and a little salt.
2. Remove the fish and skewer it onto metal or wooden skewers. Please note that if you are making use of wooden skewers, then you must have soaked them in water for up to 10minutes first. Dust these with the seasonings and spices, then chill until you are ready to cook it.
3. Now, make the salsa. Place the red onion in a bowl and cover with the lime juice then allow to sit for 5minutes. Add the remaining salsa ingredients to this mix and season. In another bowl, mix the ingredients for the chilli cream together and season.
4. Heat up the barbecue or the griddle. Cook each side of the fish for up to 2-3 mins making use of direct heat until you can see grill marks on the fish, and it feels firm. Serve the fish mango salsa, the chilli cream, extra chipotle sauce, warm corn tortillas, radishes, cabbage, Tabasco or any hot sauce of your choice. Also add lime wedges for squeezing over.

RECIPE 22: FISH WITH CHILLI, MANGO & LIME SALSA

INGREDIENTS

- Rice, to serve
- Oil (15ml//1tbsp)
- Spring Onions, sliced (2)
- Green Beans (200g//7oz)
- Lime, Juice and Zest (1 lime)
- Cajun Seasoning (1oz//2tbsp)
- Small Bunch Coriander, chopped (1)
- Ripe mango, peeled, stoned and diced (1)
- Red chilli, deseeded and finely chopped (1)
- Ripe avocado, peeled, stoned and diced (1)
- 4 whole sea bream or mackerel, descaled and cleaned (you can ask your fishmonger to do this)

STEPS

Please Note: If you are using an oven, heat to 200C/400F or fan/gas 6.

1. Make 3-4 slashes on each side of the fish, and rub the mixture of the seasoning, the lime zest and the oil into these slashes. Make sure you get right into the slashes and the cavity. Line a baking tray with foil and place the fish on it, then bake for 12-15 mins or until it is thoroughly cooked. Turn the grill to the highest and cook for 2-3 minutes more until the skin begins to char. Make sure to cover and allow it rest for a few minutes.
2. For the salsa, mix together the spring onions, the chilli, the lime juice, the coriander, the mango, the avocado and season. Boil some water in a small pan, add the beans and allow to cook for 4minutes, then drain the remaining water out.
3. Serve the fish with salsa, beans and rice. Enjoy!

RECIPE 23: SEAFOOD, PINEAPPLE & COCONUT KEBABS

INGREDIENTS

- A drizzle of Oil
- Lime Wedges, to serve
- Desiccated Coconut (85g//3oz)
- Canned Coconut Milk (200ml//7oz)
- Large, Raw King Prawns, unpeeled (16)
- Fresh Pineapples, cut into chunks (100g//4oz)
- A Mixture of boneless salmon and white fish fillets, skinned and cut into chunky pieces (500g//1.1lb)

Note: You would need: 8 skewers

STEPS

1. If your skewers are wooden, soak for 30minutes before cooking. Fire up the barbecue and allow the flames to lessen before cooking, or heat up a griddle pan until it is smoking hot.
2. Toss the coconut milk, the fish, the prawns, and some seasoning into a bowl. Thread these onto a skewer alongside the pineapple chunks. Tip the desiccated coconuts into a plate and roll the fish kebabs in it one-by-one, pressing them on the coconut to ensure that it sticks.
3. Dab the kebabs with a little oil and cook on each side for up to 3-4 minutes until the prawns turn pink and the fish is thoroughly cooked.

Serve with lime wedges and enjoy!

RECIPE 24: SKEWERED SARDINES WITH TARTARE DRESSING

INGREDIENTS

- Olive Oil (60ml//4tbsp)
- Lemon, zest and juice (1)
- Dill, finely chopped (a small bunch)
- Wooden Skewers, soaked in water (8)
- Parsley, finely chopped (a small bunch)
- Capers, drained and chopped (15ml//1tbsp)
- Cornichon, drained and finely chopped (30ml//2tbsp)
- Sardines, cleaned, gutted and heads cut off – you can ask your fishmonger to do this (12)

STEPS

1. Pour half of the lemon juice and 1tbsp of olive oil over the sardines, and rub these into the fish's cavity and its skin. Lay 2-3 of the sardines' side-by-side (depending on how big they are) and thread a skewer through the tail end and another through the head end making sure they are packed closely together.
2. To make the Tartare dressing, combine the Cornichons, the Dill, the Parsley, Capers, the Lemon zest, what is left of the Lemon Juice, the oil, and some seasoning. Then set this aside.
3. Season the sardines carefully and with the same care lift them onto the barbecue which should already be hot. Cook each side for about 3-4minutes and carefully lift the skewers to turn them over and transfer to a serving plate.
4. Scoop out a little dressing and serve the rest on the side.

RECIPE 25: BARBECUED MUSSELS

INGREDIENTS

- Mussels (1kg//2.2lb)
- Crusty Bread, to serve
- Butter, softened (50g//2oz)
- White Wine (125ml//9tbsp)
- Garlic Cloves, finely sliced (2)
- Double Cream (100ml//6tbsp)
- Shallots, halved and finely sliced (2)
- Parsley, roughly chopped (1 small pack)

STEPS

1. First mix the garlic and butter with a big pinch of salt. Heat up the barbecue until the coals are ashy white. On the kitchen counter, lay a sheet of tin foil that is about 60cm long and put another foil sheet of the same size on top of it, then add a third sheet that is about 30cm long across the middle of the other sheets to make a cross shape.
2. Spread the shallots in the middle of the foil, and pile the mussels on top, use the garlic butter to make dots all over and scatter over half the parsley. Season it, and then fold the foil in at the sides to create an oval bowl shape.
3. Pour the wine into the foil bowl and properly seal it up by squeezing the foil together at the top – it must be sealed well to ensure that the mussels can steam, so if necessary, use an extra foil sheet to give a final wrap. Carefully place the parcel on the barbecue coals and allow to cook for 10minutes.
4. After the 10minutes, open the parcel and check if the mussels have opened up – be very careful because there would be hot steam billowing out. Now, pour the cream in and cover it if your barbecue has a lid and allow to cook for a few more minutes to allow the barbecue's smoky scents get in.
5. To serve, sprinkle the meal with the remaining parsley and serve with warm crusty bread. Enjoy!

RECIPE 26: MACKEREL WITH SIZZLED GARLIC, GINGER & TOMATOES

INGREDIENTS

- Garlic cloves, thinly sliced (3)
- Chinese Rice Vinegar (5ml//1tsp)
- Sunflower or Groundnut oil (30ml//2tbsp)
- Whole mackerel, gutted and cleaned (2)
- Spring Onions, finely shredded (1 bunch)
- Cherry Tomatoes, quartered (250g//9oz pack)
- Piece of ginger, finely shredded (Thumb-sized)
- Fat Red chillies, shredded and if you prefer, deseed it (2)
- Light Soy Sauce, you can add extra to serve if you wish (5ml//1tbsp)

STEPS

1. Turn on the grill to the highest heat or fire up your barbecue – depending on which you use. Slash the fish a few times on each side and season with black pepper. For 3-5minutes, barbecue or grill the fish on each side or until all sides are cooked through and charred.

2. Heat up some oil in a frying pan – you can place the pan on a frying pan rack. Fry your ginger, chillies and garlic for about 2minutes until the garlic is a light golden color. Now, turn off the heat and toss in the cherry tomatoes & the spring onions. Place the fish onto a plate and splash with the vinegar. Then spoon over the contents of the pan and splash it with soy sauce.

Enjoy!

RECIPE 27: TIKKA-STYLE FISH

INGREDIENTS

- Turmeric (2tsp//1/6tbsp)
- Olive Oil (30ml//2tbsp)
- Cumin Seed (1tbsp//3tsp)
- Plain Yogurt (90ml//6tbsp)
- Mild Chilli Powder (2tsp//1/6tbsp)
- Four garlic cloves, finely grated or crushed (4)
- Fresh Root Ginger, finely grated (30ml//2tbsp)
- Two whole sea bream or red snapper (about 900g/2lb each) OR 6 fish steaks like tuna

STEPS

1. Lacerate the skin of the whole fish, if using, on each side with a sharp knife. Add the ginger and garlic together, season with salt, then rub all over the fish. Now, mix the yoghurt alongside the spices, oil, and seasoning. Use this to coat the fish inside and out. Chill until you are ready to cook.

2. When you are ready to barbecue, cook each side of the whole fish directly on the rack – or on the foil if you are afraid of it sticking to the rack – for up to 6-8minutes or if you are using tuna steaks, cook for 3-4 minutes. Remember that the cooking time depends on how hot your barbecue is when you start, so remember to pre-heat it.

RECIPE 28: GRILLED WILD SALMON WITH ANCHOVIES, CAPERS & LENTILS

INGREDIENTS

- Lemons (4)
- Extra-Virgin Olive Oil, for drizzling
- Capers, well rinsed (8 tbsp//1/2cup)
- Salted anchovies, rinsed, filleted and dried (16)

FOR THE LENTILS

- Garlic Cloves, peeled (2)
- 2 sprigs of sage (8-10 leaves)
- Extra-Virgin Olive Oil (90ml//6tbsp)
- Small Brown Lentils, such as Castelluccio or Puy (300g//11oz)
- Fresh flat leaf parsley, finely chopped (6tbsp//1/2cup)
- One side of a wild salmon, from a 3½ kg//8lb fish, cut into 8 portions

STEPS

1. Prepare the Lentils first by tipping them into a small saucepan, covering them with water and adding sage and garlic to the mix. Allow this simmer gently for 15-20 minutes until it is tender. Then drain and discard the sage and the garlic, season this with both salt and pepper to desired taste. Then stir in the olive oil and set the Lentils aside.
2. Place the anchovies in a bowl and squeeze the juice from one lemon over them. Add freshly ground black pepper and drizzle with olive oil. The capers and parsley should be mixed in another bowl. You can choose to do this several hours ahead.
3. Preheat the griddle pan until it is very hot and season the salmon on both sides of it, then sear it skin-side down – note that if the barbecue/pan is very hot the skin won't stick. When you see it change color halfway, turn the fish and sear the other side. This process should take 2-3 minutes on each side for rare salmon, however thicker fishes would cause cooking times t0 vary.
4. Now it is time to serve! Reheat the already-prepared Lentils and place a large spoonful of it at the center of warmed plates. Top this off with the salmon with the skin-side up, then scatter the parsley, the capers and the anchovies on top. Remember to serve with the remaining lemons.

RECIPE 29: GRILLED SALMON TERIYAKI WITH CUCUMBER SALAD

INGREDIENTS

- Soy Sauce (75ml//5tbsp)
- Sunflower oil (15ml//1tbsp)
- Mirin or Dry Sherry (75ml//5tbsp)
- Golden Caster Sugar (15ml//1tbsp)
- Garlic Cloves, crushed to a paste (2)
- Frozen Boneless Salmon Fillets, skinless (4)
- Fresh Root Ginger, peeled and finely grated (1piece)

FOR THE CUCUMBER SALAD

- Small Cucumber (1)
- Soy Sauce (15ml//1tbsp)
- Rice Wine Vinegar (15ml//1tbsp)
- Golden Caster Sugar (8tbsp//½ tsp)
- Toasted Sesame Seeds (1tbsp//3tsp)

STEPS

1. Heat the grill to high and brush a strong baking tray with oil. Using a large bowl, mix the garlic, ginger, sugar, mirin and soy together until the sugar has dissolved. Toss the frozen salmon into the soy mix until it is fully coated and tip whatever remains of the marinade into a small saucepan. Allow this to simmer.

2. Place the tray about 4inches away from the heat and grill for close to 20minutes. Make sure you brush the fish every few minutes with the simmering marinade until it is evenly cooked and glazed. Note that if the fillets are thick, you might have to turn them on their sides to ensure they cook evenly. Remove the fish from the grill and simmer the marinade until it is sticky. Pour this over the cooked salmon.

3. To make the cucumber salad, make use of a swivel blade peeler to peel the cucumber into slices. Make the dressing by mixing the sesame seeds, the soy sauce, sugar with the vinegar. Toss the cucumber with the dressing and serve with the boiled rice and the salmon.

RECIPE 30: BAKED SEA BASS WITH LEMONGRASS & GINGER

INGREDIENTS

- Limes (2)
- Olive Oil (30ml//2tbsp)
- Garlic Cloves, halved (2)
- Small Chillies, halved (2)
- Runny Honey (5ml//1 tsp)
- Fresh Ginger, peeled and cut into thin strips (3cm piece)
- Lemongrass stalks, cut diagonally into 2½ cm pieces (3)
- One Whole Sea Bass (about 1.4kg/3lb), gutted and cleaned
- Two kaffir lime leaves (substitute with a few strips of lime peel if kaffir lime leaves are unavailable)

STEPS

1. Start off with preheating the oven to 400F/200C/gas 6. Clean the sea bass in-and-out making sure to wash it well and pat it dry with kitchen paper. Scour across the fish and through the skin about 4-5 times on each side before laying the fish on a large piece of foil that has been previously oiled. The foil should be big enough to loosely wrap up the fish.
2. Put in the garlic, chillies, ginger, and lemongrass into a mortar. Add 1tbsp of oil, some honey, squeeze in the juice from one of the limes and pound together until everything is bruised – note that there is no need to grind it finely.
3. Put the lemongrass, chillies, garlic and ginger into a mortar with the honey and 1 tbsp of the oil. Squeeze in the juice of one of the limes. Bash a few times with the pestle until everything's bruised – there's no need to grind it finely.
4. Season the fish in-and-out then scrape half of the pounded mixture on the fish. Add the last of the oil and rub everything in, making sure you push it properly into the cuts.

BURGER RECIPES

RECIPE 31: SOUTHWEST BURGERS

INGREDIENTS

- Salt (4g//3/4tsp)
- Lettuce Leaves (8)
- Chili Powder (1tsp)
- Pepper (3g//1/2tsp)
- Garlic Powder (3/4tsp)
- Large tomato, sliced (1)
- Ground Cumin (23g//4tsp)
- Bulk Pork Sausage (340g//3/4lb)
- Monterey Jack Cheese (8 slices)
- Mayonnaise or mustard, optional
- Hamburger Buns, split & toasted (8)
- Ripe Avocados, peeled and sliced (1-2)
- Lean ground beef (900g//2lb)
- Chopped Green Chilies (1 can//4oz)

STEPS

1. Using a large bowl, combine the Green Chilies, the Cumin, the Chilli, Garlic, Salt and Pepper and mix thoroughly. Crumble the sausage and the beef into the mixture and mix properly. Spread this mixture into eight patties.
2. Grill each side of the patties over medium heat for about 5minutes, or you can use a thermometer that reads 160°. Make sure that the juices run clear and top each burger with a cheese slice. Grill for 1-2 minutes more, or until the cheese begins to melt.
3. Serve this awesomeness on buns with the tomato, lettuce, mayonnaise/ mustard and avocado if desired.

RECIPE 32: JALAPENO SWISS BURGERS

INGREDIENTS

- Swiss cheese (4 slices)
- 1 small onion, finely chopped
- Ground Beef (908g//2lb)
- Lettuce leaves and ketchup, optional
- Hamburger Buns, split and toasted (4)
- Pickled Jalapeno Peppers, seeded and finely chopped (2-3)

STEPS

1. Shape the beef into 8 thin patties, and top 4 of these with jalapenos, onions and cheese. Top the remaining 4 patties and press the edges firmly to ensure it is sealed. Grill the now-covered patties on either side over medium heat for about 8-9 minutes, or use a thermometer that reads 160°. Make sure the juices run clear, and serve on buns. If you wish for toppings, do not hesitate to add them.

RECIPE 33: CLASSIC GRILLED BURGERS

INGREDIENTS

- A-1 sauce (2tbsp)
- Seasoned Salt (2tbsp)
- Freshly Ground Black Pepper (1tsp)
- Room-Temperature Water (1/4 cup)
- Ground Beef, preferably not extra lean) (908g//2lb)

STEPS

1. Using a medium bowl, mix all the ingredients together until they are thoroughly mixed. Form the beef into patties, making sure they are 1/2inch thick and about 1/4inch larger in diameter than the buns you would be using. Now, refrigerate the patties until ready to grill.
2. Over medium-high heat and on a preheated grill, cook the burgers until they are cooked to your liking, most people tend to cook for up to 6minutes. In the last two minutes of grilling, butter the inside of the bun and place it on the grill to toast until the burgers finish cooking.

RECIPE 34: BBQ BURGERS

INGREDIENTS

FOR THE PATTIES

- Salt (1 tbs)
- Ground Beef (1 kg//2.2lb)
- Black Pepper (1 tbsp)
- 3 tbsp hickory BBQ sauce
- Garlic Cloves, chopped finely (2)
- Medium Onion, chopped into small pieces (1)

TO MAKE BURGER

- Dijon Mustard
- Burger Buns (12)
- Chilli Garlic Ketchup
- Large Onions, cut these into rings (3)
- Tomatoes, cut this into rings (400g//0.9lb)
- Large Lettuce Head, washed and separated (1)
- 12 slices of cheese (you can use any brand of your choice)

STEPS

1. Using a large mixing bowl, put the garlic, pepper, onions, BBQ sauce and the Ground Beef together. Mix these properly until the BBQ sauce is consistently distributed through the beef. Scoop the patty portion with your hands and roll these into a ball, then gently flatten them out to create circular shapes.
2. For 10minutes (if you are going for a rare burger) or 12-15 minutes (if you are going for a medium), cook both sides of the patties thoroughly. And while the second side of the patty is cooking, place a slice of cheese on it so that it melts slightly.
3. For nothing more than 2-3minutes, heat up the burger buns on the BBQ and spread the Dijon mustard on the bottom bun. Now, put the burger patty on the bun before adding lettuce, tomatoes and onions. Remember that you can spread the chilli garlic ketchup on the top bun, or you can choose to serve it on the side.

RECIPE 35: BOLD HONEY-BARBECUE BURGER

INGREDIENTS

- Honey (1tbsp)
- Fresh lettuce (4)
- Slices tomato (4)
- Hamburger Buns (4)
- Garlic Powder (½tsp)
- Melted Butter (2tbsp)
- Cayenne Pepper (½tsp)
- Barbecue Sauce (¾ cup)
- Steak Seasoning (2tbsp)
- Ground Beef (1pound//2cups)
- Green Onions, chopped (½ cup)
- Thick slices bacon, cooked crisp (8)
- Borden® American Cheese Singles (4 slices)
- Frozen onion rings, prepared according to package directions (8)

STEPS

1. Mix the garlic powder, the green onions, the cayenne pepper and the ground beef together, and form the result into 4 patties. Sprinkle both sides of each patty with steak seasoning, then cover and keep to chill. If you want to make these in advance, you can do that. Using melted butter, brush the buns and set this aside. Also mix the honey and the BBQ sauce in a small bowl and set aside.
2. Preheat the grill to medium-high heat and grill the burgers to an internal temperature of 160°F//74°C for about 4-6minutes for each side. Just 2minutes before the burgers get grilled, grill the buns with the buttered-side down until it is golden brown. Place the Borden® American Cheese Singles on the burgers to melt.
3. Serve each burger on a buttered bun and top it 2 slices of crisp bacon and onion rings, honey barbeque sauce, lettuce and tomato.

RECIPE 36: CAJUN CHICKEN & PINEAPPLE BURGER

INGREDIENTS

- Drizzle of olive oil
- Chicken Breasts (4)
- Lettuce leaves (a few)
- Red Onion, thinly sliced (1)
- Soured Cream (34g//2tbsp)
- Cheddar, grated (50g//1.8oz)
- Cajun Seasoning (34g//2tbsp)
- Pineapple Rings, from a can (4)
- Burger Buns, split and toasted (4)

STEPS

1. Line a baking tray with foil and heat up the grill to medium-high. Place the chicken between 2 sheets of cling film and bash it with a rolling pin until you achieve an even thickness. Now rub the oil, some seasoning, and the Cajun mix all over the chicken and place them on the baking tray. Grill them for 10minutes, turning them after 5minutes. Top each chicken breast with some grated cheese and a pineapple ring, grill it again and cook for another 2-3 minutes until the cheese bubbles and has turned golden and the chicken is properly cooked.
2. Add a little soured cream over the base of each bun, then add lettuce, a chicken breast, sliced red onion, and pop the top on.

RECIPE 37: SMOKY MUSHROOM BURGERS WITH ROASTED GARLIC MAYO

INGREDIENTS

- Large Flat Mushrooms (4)
- Red Onions, thinly sliced (3)
- Sherry Vinegar (15ml//1tbsp)
- Smoked Paprika (11.4g//2tsp)
- Fresh Breadcrumbs (50g//1.8oz)
- Golden Caster Sugar (17g//1tbsp)
- Sundried Tomato Paste (6g//1tsp)
- Olive Oil, get some extra for frying (15ml//1tbsp)
- Thyme, leaves picked and chopped (½small pack)
- Roasted Red Peppers (from a jar), finely chopped (2)

FOR THE GARLIC MAYO

- Garlic Cloves, unpeeled (3)
- Good-Quality Mayonnaise (50g//1.8oz)

TO SERVE

- Salad Leaves
- Crusty Bread Rolls (4)
- Cheddar or Manchego, grated (25g//0.9oz)

STEPS

1. Fire up the barbecue!
2. To make the garlic mayo, start by using a foil parcel to wrap the garlic cloves. Place this on a hot spot of the barbecue and cook it for up to 20minutes until it is really soft. However, if you are using an oven, bake the garlic gloves in a hot oven for 20-30minutes.

3. Allow it to cool before squeezing the cloves out of their skins and mashing them with a fork. Mix this garlic purée with the with the mayonnaise, and allow to chill until you are ready to serve.
4. Now, to make the rest of this amazing meal. Remove the stalks from the middle of the mushrooms and finely chop them. Heat a drizzle of oil on the barbecue, hob or in a pan; then add the stalks and fry them for a few minutes until they are soft and golden. Now add the breadcrumbs, the tomato paste, the peppers, thyme, paprika, and some seasoning and cook these for 5 more minutes. Afterwards, set this and allow to cool for a little while. With a little oil, rub the mushroom caps, season them and top each one with 1/4 of the mixture. It can be chilled for up to a day.
5. In another frying pan, barbecue or hob, heat up a little oil and add the onions. Cook it for 15minutes until it is soft and golden, now add the vinegar, the sugar, and some seasoning, and cook for 5 more minutes until it is sticky and caramelized. This can be chilled for up to 2 days.
6. With the stuffed side facing up, put the mushrooms on the barbecue and cover with foil or close the lid and allow to cook for 20minutes until it is soft and properly cooked. Pay close attention to the heat and move to the upper shelf if the mushrooms' bottoms begin to burn. Take the rolls apart and heat these on the barbecue, too. On each roll spread some garlic mayo, top with salad leaves, a filled mushroom, some sticky onions, and a grating of cheese.

RECIPE 38: HARISSA TURKEY BURGERS

INGREDIENTS

- Red Peppers (2)
- Lemon, juiced (1)
- Rocket (150g//5.3oz)
- Rose Harissa (60ml//4tbsp)
- Rapeseed Oil (30ml//2tbsp)
- Cooked Beetroot, grated (3)
- Small Bunch Parsley, finely chopped
- Large Garlic Cloves, finely grated (2)

FOR THE SAUCE

- Medium-sized Courgette (1)
- Low-Fat Mayonnaise (30ml//2tbsp)
- Small Bunch Dill, finely chopped (½)
- Fat-Free Greek Yogurt (60ml//4tbsp)
- Lean Turkey Breast mince (500g//1.1lb)
- Whole Meal Seeded Buns, toasted – to serve (4)
- Coriander Seeds, toasted and crushed (6g//1tsp)
- Pouch OR Cooked mixed grains (250g//9oz, either way)

STEPS

1. Cook the grains according to pack instructions. Leave to cool, then tip into a bowl and use your hands to mix in the turkey, garlic, coriander, harissa and parsley. Shape into four patties. Cover and chill.
2. To make the sauce, coarsely grate the courgette, discarding the seeds, then wrap in a clean cloth and squeeze out any liquid. Put in a bowl and mix with the dill, yogurt, 2 tbsp water and the mayonnaise.
3. Put the peppers on the barbecue and cook for 10-15 mins or until blistered and starting to char. Or, heat a grill to its highest setting and grill for 15-20 mins, turning halfway. Leave to cool a little, then peel and cut into strips.
4. Toss the rocket with half the oil and lemon juice.
5. Brush the burgers with the remaining oil and cook for 6 mins each side. Alternatively, heat the oil in a frying pan over a medium heat and fry for 6 mins each side. Serve with the sauce, peppers, beetroot, buns and salad so everyone can assemble their own burger.

RECIPE 39: ROSEMARY & GARLIC LAMB BURGER

INGREDIENTS

FOR THE BURGERS

- Needles
- Mince (10% fat)
- Lean Lamb (1kg//2.2lb)
- Garlic Cloves, chopped (2)
- Rosemary, finely chopped (23g//4tsp)

TO SERVE

- Mayonnaise
- Sliced Tomatoes
- Good Handful Rocket
- Ciabatta rolls or French bread
- Red Onions, sliced and tossed (3)
- Balsamic Vinegar & Olive Oil (15ml//1tbsp each)

STEPS

1. Mash the garlic, rosemary, 1 tsp salt and ½ -1 tsp pepper with a pestle and mortar to make a paste. Add this to the lamb and stir well with your hands. Don't overburden the meat or you will toughen it.
2. Split the mixture into 8 parts, then sharpen into round burgers. If eating immediately, heat up a barbecue or grill and cook for about 8-10 mins. Turn frequently, until it cooks to your liking. Divide the rolls or bread, toast lightly on one side, add mayo spread, then add the burgers and the balsamic onions, tomatoes, and rocket.

RECIPE 40: BARBECUED BURGERS

INGREDIENTS

TO MAKE THE BURGERS

- Honey (3oz//1/4cup)
- Sugar (3tbsp//1/3cup)
- Salt (15drops//1/4 tsp)
- Ketchup (8fl.oz//1cup)
- Molasses (3oz//1/4cup)
- Pepper (6drops//1/8 tsp)
- Liquid Smoke (15drops//1/4 tsp)
- Prepared Mustard (11.4g//2tsp)
- Packed Brown Sugar (8tbsp//1/2 cup)
- Worcestershire Sauce (5ml-5.5ml//1-11/2 tsp)

SAUCE

- Salt (6drops//1/8 tsp)
- Toppings of your choice
- Hamburger Buns, split (6)
- Pepper (15drops//1/4 tsp)
- Large Egg, lightly beaten (1)
- Quick-Cooking Oats (1/3 cup)
- Onion salt (15drops//1/4 tsp)
- Garlic salt (15drops//1/4 tsp)
- ground beef (460-680g//1-11/2lb)

STEPS

1. In a small saucepan, combine the first 10 ingredients. Bring to a boil. Remove from the heat. Put to a side 1 cup barbecue sauce to serve with burgers.
2. In a large bowl, mix together the oats, onion salt, the eggs, garlic salt, 1/4 cup of what remains of the barbecue sauce, pepper, and salt. Crush the beef over mixture and mix it thoroughly. Shape the mixture into six patties.
3. Barbecue, covered, over medium heat for 6-8 minutes. Do for each side until a thermometer reads 160°, Bast with 1/2 cup barbecue sauce during the last 5 minutes. Serve on buns with toppings of your choice and reserved barbecue sauce.

BARBECUE SAUCE RECIPES

RECIPE 41: ST. LOUIS BARBECUE SAUCE

INGREDIENTS

- Cayenne (3g//1/2tsp)
- Salt (15drops//1/4 tsp)
- Water (4fl.oz//1/2cup)
- Ketchup (16fl.oz//2cups)
- Brown Sugar (75g//1/3cup)
- Garlic Powder (17g//1tbsp)
- Onion Powder (17g//1tbsp)
- Yellow Mustard (30ml//2tbsp)
- Apple Cider Vinegar (110g//1/3cup)

STEPS

1. Mix all the ingredients in a medium saucepan, over low heat. Occasionally stir and allow to simmer for up to 20 minutes. Note that the sauce ought to be thin, but not watery. Remove the sauce from the heat and allow to cool for about 20-30 minutes.
2. The sauce can be used immediately it cooks or you can chill for a day. To chill, place it in an airtight container and store in the refrigerator. It can be stored for up to a week after preparation in a refrigerator and up to 3-4months in a freezer.

Tip: This sauce goes well with ribs, pork chops, pork steaks, hot dogs, burgers, steaks, chicken, etc. and it can also be a dipping sauce.

RECIPE 42: TEXAS BBQ SAUCE

INGREDIENTS

- Salt, to taste
- Pepper, to taste
- Butter (20g//1/4cup)
- Water (8fl.oz// 1cup)
- Honey (30ml//2tbsp)
- Paprika (15ml//1tbsp)
- Ketchup (8fl.oz// 1cup)
- Chili Powder (11.4g//2tsp)
- Beef Bouillon (1tsp), cubed
- Spicy Mustard (30ml//2tbsp)
- Onion, minced (20g//1/4cup)
- Celery Stalks, chopped (3)
- Garlic Cloves, minced (2)
- Worcestershire Sauce (3tbsp)
- Apple Cider Vinegar (45g//1/2cup)

STEPS

1. Using a medium-sized saucepan and over medium-low heat, melt the butter and add the celery and onion to the mix. Cook this for up to 4-5 minutes, and until the celery and the onions are soft. Add the minced garlic and cook for nothing more than 15 - 20 seconds.
2. Now, add the bouillon cube and the water, stir in the water until the bouillon is dissolved. Begin to add the remaining ingredients, the ketchup, the spicy mustard, the honey, paprika, chili powder, the Worcestershire sauce, the cider vinegar, the salt and the pepper to taste. Simmer this on low for up to 15 minutes and stir occasionally.
3. When it is ready, remove the sauce and turn of the heat. Allow it to cool for up to 15minutes and pour into a food processor or a blender, and blend until it is smooth enough, this should take about 15-20 seconds.
4. The sauce should be used immediately or stored in an airtight container and kept in a refrigerator. It cannot be kept for more than 7days though. And before the next use, you have to warm it slightly.

RECIPE 43: SOUTHERN BARBECUE SAUCE

INGREDIENTS

- Bay Leaf (1)
- Sugar (2tbsp)
- Butter (2tbsp)
- Garlic, minced (1)
- Water (4fl.oz//1/2cup)
- Ketchup (12fl.oz//11/2cups)
- Cider Vinegar (90ml//6tbsp)
- Vegetable Oil (45ml//3tbsp)
- Tabasco sauce (45g//1/4 tsp)
- Teaspoon paprika (5ml//1tsp)
- Cayenne Pepper (45g//1/4 tsp)
- Worcestershire sauce (30ml//2tbsp)
- Lemon juice, from a large lemon (45ml//3tbsp)

STEPS

1. In a medium saucepan, heat up the vegetable oil and add the minced garlic to it. Allow to cook for between 15-30 seconds until it becomes fragrant. Now, add the Worcestershire sauce, the cayenne pepper, the cider vinegar, the ketchup, the Tabasco sauce, the lemon juice, the paprika, the sugar, the water and the bay leaf. Please do not avoid the butter now.
2. Allow the sauce to simmer over a medium-low heat for between 8-10 minutes, stirring occasionally. Watch to see if it is burning, and lower the temperature when necessary. When it is ready, remove the pan from the heat and stir in the butter. Once the butter is thoroughly melted through, allow the sauce cool for between 10-15 minutes before using it.
3. If you are preparing the sauce in advance, cool it for 30minutes and store in an airtight container in a refrigerator. It can be stored for up to 4 or 5 days after preparation.

RECIPE 44: BBQ RUM SAUCE

INGREDIENTS

- Onion, chopped (1/2)
- Paprika (1tbsp//15ml)
- Vinegar (2tbsp//30ml)
- Olive Oil (1tbsp//15ml)
- Molasses (1tbsp//15ml)
- Dark Rum (1/4cup//60ml)
- Brown Sugar (1/4cup//120ml)
- Garlic, minced (1/2cup//2Cloves)
- Worcestershire sauce (1tbsp//15ml)
- Tomato Sauce (2 cans//8-ounce/240ml)
- Green Chilies (medium heat) (1can//8oz//240ml)

STEPS

1. Pour the Olive Oil in a medium-sized saucepan and place over medium heat. Add the onion and garlic and sauté until it is opaque. Add every other ingredient, except the rum and mix well. Allow this mix to boil lightly and then turn off the heat. Now, pour in the run and stir until it has been well-absorbed into the sauce. When the sauce has cooled down, pour into a blender or use a hand blender to blend until you have a smooth puree.

Serve and enjoy!

RECIPE 45: BEST BBQ SAUCE

INGREDIENTS

- Salt (2tsp//10ml)
- Sugar (1/4 cup//60ml)
- Water (1cup//240ml)
- Ketchup (1cup//240ml)
- Garlic, minced (3cloves)
- Lemon, juice and zest (1/2)
- Onion, coarsely chopped (1)
- Cayenne Pepper (1tsp//5ml)
- Cider Vinegar (1/2 cup//120ml)
- Vegetable Oil (1tbsp//15ml)
- Ginger, fresh grated (2tsp//10 ml)

STEPS

1. Using a saucepan, over medium heat, heat up the oil and add garlic, onion, and ginger. Sauté until the onion is translucent. Now, stir in the ketchup, the vinegar, the lemon juice and zest, the cayenne pepper, the ketchup, the water, salt and sugar. Reduce the heat to a low simmer and cook for another 25 minutes.

RECIPE 46: BARBECUE SAUCE

INGREDIENTS

- Olive Oil (1tbsp)
- Onion, finely chopped (1)
- Brown Sugar (85g//1/2cups)
- Malt Vinegar (45ml//3tbsp)
- Tomato Purée (15ml//1tbsp)
- Garlic, finely chopped (3 cloves)
- Worcestershire Sauce (30ml//2tbsp)
- Canned Tomatoes, chopped (400g//0.9lb)

STEPS

1. Heat up the oil in a saucepan and add the onions. Once it starts to fry, allow to cook over a gentle heat of 4-5 mins, until it is softened. Once softened, add the remaining ingredients, season to your taste, and stir. Allow to the boil, then reduce the heat and simmer for 20-30 mins, until it is thickened. To get a smooth sauce, simply blend the mixture in a food processor or use a hand blender for a only few seconds.

RECIPE 47: ALABAMA WHITE BBQ SAUCE

INGREDIENTS

- Water (15ml//3tsp)
- Hot Sauce (3g//¼ tsp)
- Kosher Salt (3g//½tsp)
- Garlic Powder (3g//½tsp)
- Mayonnaise (40g//1 cup)
- Onion Powder (3g//½tsp)
- Worcestershire sauce (5ml//1tsp)
- Apple Cider Vinegar (2 3/4 fl. oz//⅓ cup)
- Freshly Ground Black Pepper (3g//½tsp)

STEPS

1. In a small bowl, stir the Worcestershire sauce, mayonnaise, vinegar, garlic powder, water, hot sauce, the onion powder, salt and pepper. Stir properly. You can choose to serve immediately or keep it in a refrigerator for up to 3days.

RECIPE 48: SWEET AND SMOKE HOMEMADE BBQ SAUCE

INGREDIENTS

- Paprika (12g//2tsp)
- Cayenne (6g//1tsp)
- Water (2fl.oz//1/4 cup)
- Ketchup (8fl.oz//1cup)
- Olive Oil (45ml//3tbsp)
- Chili Powder (6g//1tsp)
- Garlic, minced (2 cloves)
- Smoked Paprika (6g//1tsp)
- Brown Sugar (4tbsp//1/4 cup)
- Apple Cider Vinegar (4tbsp//1/4 cup)

STEPS

1. In a small saucepan, and over medium heat, heat the oil. When the oil is hot enough, add the minced garlic and sauté for 2minutes. Add the remaining ingredients and allow to cook for 3minutes. Now, reduce the heat to low and allow to simmer for 15 minutes until it thickens.

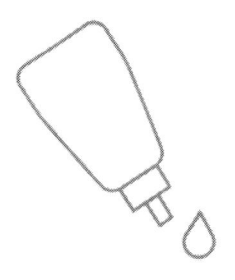

RECIPE 49: BBQ SAUCE – WITHOUT KETCHUP

INGREDIENTS

- Sea Salt (1/2 tsp)
- Black Pepper (1.4g//1/4tsp)
- Garlic Powder (1.4g//1/4tsp)
- Onion Powder (1.4g//1/4tsp)
- Apple Cider Vinegar (4tbsp//1/4cup)
- Cayenne Pepper to taste (a pinch)
- Blackstrap Molasses or Maple Syrup (8tbsp//1/2cup)
- Organic Tomato Sauce, preferably homemade, or jarred (16fl.oz//2cups)

STEPS

1. Mix all the ingredients in a saucepan, over medium heat. Boil for only 1 minute, then reduce heat and simmer for 20 minutes. When it is ready, pour into a mason jar and allow it to cool. Then, seal and store in the fridge. Once opened, it will last about 3-4 weeks.

RECIPE 50: GRAPE JELLY BBQ SAUCE - APPLE JELLY BBQ SAUCE

INGREDIENTS

- BBQ sauce (2 parts)
- Apple jelly or Grape jelly (1 part)

STEPS

1. Over medium-low heat, mix the BBQ Sauce and the jelly in a pan and stir occasionally until they are thoroughly mixed. Put it down and allow to cool, then serve or refrigerate.

DESSERT & SNACK RECIPES

RECIPE 51: GRILLED PEACH MELBA

INGREDIENTS

- Sugar (1tbsp)
- Raspberries (1/2pt.)
- Large Ripe Peaches (2)
- Vanilla Ice Cream (12fl. oz//11/2cups)

STEPS

1. Set up the outdoor grill for direct grilling on medium heat. Place the peach halves on the now hot grill grate and cook for up between 5-6 minutes, turn them over once and cook until the peaches are lightly charred and tender.
2. Prepare the sauce in a bowl by using a fork to mash half of the raspberries with sugar. Stir in remaining raspberries.
3. To serve, place a peach half in each of 4 dessert bowls and top with ice cream and raspberry sauce.

RECIPE 52: ROAST WHOLE PINEAPPLE WITH BLACK PEPPER & RUM

INGREDIENTS

- Light Muscovado Sugar (100g//3.5oz)
- Pineapple, peeled, top leaves left on (1)
- Butter, cut into small pieces (50g//1.8oz)
- Chilli Flakes, plus extra to serve (6g//1tsp)

FOR THE RUM CREAM

- White Rum (30ml//2tbsp)
- Canned Coconut Cream (160g//6oz)

STEPS

1. Heat up the oven to 180C/350F/gas 4.
2. In a large roasting, mix the chilli, the sugar, and 1 tsp of cracked pepper tin. Roll the pineapple in this mix, allow it to lay in the excess and dot the top with the pieces of butter. If any pieces of butter fall into the tin, they will be used for basting.
3. Roast the pineapple for up to 30minutes and baste every 10minutes with the buttery juices, do this until the pineapple is sticky and golden. Now, remove the dish from the oven and leave to cool slightly. While it cools, make the rum cream.
4. Whip the coconut cream into soft peaks, then pour in the rum. Just before serving, baste the pineapple again, and bring it to the table whole in the roasting tin and sprinkled with some extra chilli flakes. Carve the pineapple into wedges or slices, as you please, and serve with any extra sauce from the tin and a large dollop of the cream.

RECIPE 53: GRILLED DONUT ICE CREAM SANDWICHES

INGREDIENTS

- Whipped Cream
- Maraschino Cherries (4)
- Vanilla Ice Cream (8 scoops)
- Glazed Donuts, cut in half (4)
- Chocolate syrup, for drizzling

STEPS

1. Preheat the grill pan or the grill to high heat and grill the donut halves, glazed side down, until charred, about 1 minute. Set aside to cool. Put 2 scoops of vanilla ice cream in between each donut sandwich and press down. Top each donut with a drizzle of chocolate syrup, whipped cream, and of course, a cherry on top!

Serve and enjoy!

RECIPE 54: GRILLED PINEAPPLE SUNDAES

INGREDIENTS

- Pineapple Slices (4)
- Vanilla Ice Cream (4 scoops)
- Dulce de leche, for drizzling
- Sweetened Shredded Coconut, toasted (2 tbsp)

STEPS

1. Fire up the grill on high heat and grill the pineapple until it is charred on all sides, 1 minut per side is enough to achieve this. At the top of each pile of pineapple slices, place some vanilla ice cream and drizzle with some caramel or some dulce de leche or. Top with the shredded coconut and serve immediately!

RECIPE 55: SPANISH MELON WITH SERRANO HAM

INGREDIENTS

- Ham, thin Serrano (12 slices)
- Ripe melon, honeydew (1/2)

STEPS

1. Rinse the melon and pat it dry. Cut it in half, deseed it and cut away the rind. Cut the melon into 1 1/2" cubes. Cut the ham slices into halves and wrap each melon cube with a ham. Use the toothpicks to hold the hams in place. Serve cold or at least at room temperature.

VEGETARIAN RECIPES

RECIPE 56: SWEET POTATOES WITH RED PEPPER & HALLOUMI

INGREDIENTS

- 1 lemon, halved
- Butter (optional)
- 4 medium sweet potatoes
- 1 tbsp olive oil (15g//0.53 oz)
- 4 fat strips grilled red pepper
- 8 mint leaves, finely chopped
- Small bunch parsley, chopped
- 225g halloumi, cut into 4 slices (1cup//7.9oz)

STEPS

1. Rub each sweet potato with a little oil and salt, then wrap in a double layer of foil.
2. Empty the oil into a bowl and stir the mint into it. Add the halloumi and toss until it is well-coated in the minty oil, then wrap each piece in a strip of pepper. Cut four lengths of foil about 1cm wide and wrap one around the middle of each parcel to hold them together. Skewers can be used in this situation, but you must ensure you do not split the cheese.
3. Heat the barbecue. Once the coals glow red, place the potatoes directly on them. Cook for 30 mins, turning halfway. Unwrap a potato and check if it is cooked thoroughly. If not, rewrap and allow to cook longer, checking every 10 mins. Alternatively, bake in the oven at 200C/180C fan/gas 6 for 50 mins-1 hr.
4. Place the pepper parcels on the barbecue or a griddle pan for 3-4 mins each side or until the pepper chars and cheese melts a bit. Remove from the grill and unwind the foil or remove the skewers. Split the potatoes, add butter if you like, then lay a parcel in the center of each. Add a squeeze of lemon and scatter over some parsley to serve.

RECIPE 57: GRIDDLED VEGETABLES WITH MELTING AUBERGINES

INGREDIENTS

- Large Aubergine (1)
- Kalamata olives, halved (8)
- Thyme Leaves (11.4g//2tsp)
- Rapeseed Oil (15ml//1 tbsp)
- Lemon, zested and juiced (½)
- Omega Seed mix (20ml//4tsp)
- Large Onion, thickly sliced (1)
- Courgettes, sliced on the angle (2)
- Garlic Cloves (3), 1 crushed, 2 chopped
- Chopped Parsley, plus extra to serve (2tbsp)
- Large tomatoes, cut each into 3 thick slices (2)
- Red Pepper, deseeded and cut into quarters (1)
- Extra virgin olive oil, plus a little for drizzling (5ml//1tsp)

STEPS

1. Start off with grilling the Aubergine, making sure that you turn it frequently until all sides of it are soft and the skin has been blistered, this process should last for about 8-10 minutes. Or if you have a gas hob, you could cook the Aubergine directly over the flame to make the process faster.
2. When the Aubergine is cool enough to handle, remove the skin and chop the flesh away finely. Mix the chopped skin with the lemon juice, 1 chopped garlic clove, 1tsp of extra virgin olive oil, 1tsp of parsley and the seeds. The remaining parsley should be mixed with the remaining chopped garlic and the lemon zest.
3. Also, mix the thyme, the rapeseed oil and the crushed garlic and toss with the vegetables, making sure that you keep the onions as slices rather than breaking them up into rings. Heat up a large girdle pan and char the vegetables until they are tender and marked with lines, the tomatoes will need the least amount of time to char.
4. Place these in plates with the Aubergine purée and the olives, drizzle over a little extra olive oil and scatter the garlic, lemon zest and parsley on it. Now enjoy!

RECIPE 58: BUTTER-BASTED BBQ CABBAGE

INGREDIENTS

- Butter (100g//3.5oz)
- Garlic Cloves, grated (4)
- Muscovado sugar (1tbsp)
- Lime, finely zested and juiced (1)
- Green Chillies, finely chopped (2)
- Small Bunch of Coriander, chopped (1)
- Medium-sized Savoy or King cabbage, outer leaves should be kept on (1)

STEPS

1. Fire up a lidded barbecue and allow the flames die down and the coals to become ashen. Mount the coals on one side of barbecue. If you are using an oven, heat it 180C/160C fan/gas 4//350F
2. Clean the cabbage carefully and ensure there is no grit or soil on it. Beat the butter with the other ingredients and add a pinch of salt. Open the cabbage's outer leaves to expose the main ball, spread these leaves out and make a few big cuts into the heart of the cabbage. Smear butter over the middle of it and draw these leaves back up. Secure the cabbage with a string to ensure the leaves do not fall off.
3. Place the cabbage in a roasting tin and cook it for 1hr 15 mins, or until the outer leaves are charred and an inserted skewer does not offer too much resistance. Now, remove the cabbage and cut off the string, take off the outer leaves to expose the cooked middle. Cut this middle into wedges and baste with the butter in the tray while it is still warm to ensure the cabbage soaks up the flavors.

RECIPE 59: BARBECUE SESAME SWEET POTATOES

INGREDIENTS

- Lime, juiced (1)
- Green chilli, sliced (1)
- Soy Sauce (45ml//3tbsp)
- Garlic Clove, chopped (1)
- Vegetable Oil (45ml//3tbsp)
- Ginger, chopped (17g//1tbsp)
- Sesame Oil, toasted (5ml//1tsp)
- Plain Peanuts, crushed (50g//1.8oz)
- Spring onions, washed and chopped (½ bunch)
- Sesame Seeds, black seeds if possible (17g//1tbsp)
- Sweet Potatoes, washed and cut into wedges (6)

STEPS

1. Fire up a lidded barbecue and allow the flames to die down and the coals to turn ashen, now place the coals on one side in a mound. If you are using an oven, heat to 180C/160C fan/gas 4//350F. Place the sweet potatoes on a large tray and drizzle with 1 tbsp of the vegetable oil, then season and toss together. Cook for 25 minutes until it is charred and soft.

2. Now, whisk the lime juice, ginger, soy, garlic, and the remaining oils in a bowl. Baste the potatoes with some of this sauce and return them to the barbecue for another 30-40 minutes, basting while they cook. Once they are sticky and glazed, remove them and sprinkle the peanuts and the sesame seeds on them. Leave the potatoes to cool slightly, remove the wedges from the tray and place in a salad bowl. Sprinkle the chilli and spring onions to serve. Enjoy your meal!

RECIPE 60: BARBECUE BAKED SWEET POTATOES

INGREDIENTS

- Olive oil (20ml//4 tsp)
- Spring onion, sliced (1)
- Medium sweet potatoes (8)
- Greek yogurt (60ml//4tbsp)

STEPS

1. First rub each potato with a little salt and oil before wrapping in a double layer of foil. Fire up the barbecue and when the barbecue coals are glowing red, place the potatoes directly on them. Cook the potatoes for about 15 minutes, turn them with tongs and cook for 15 minutes more.
2. To check if it is thoroughly cooked through, remove one to unwrap and check. When it is thoroughly cooked through, peel back the top of the foil from each potato, split them open and top each sweet potato with a spoonful of yogurt and a few slices of spring onions

Printed in Great Britain
by Amazon